WHY SMART PEOPLE HURT

JOURNAL

Books by Eric Maisel

Why Smart, Creative and Highly Sensitive People Hurt

Why Smart Teens Hurt

The Great Book of Journaling

Redesign Your Mind

Everyday You

Affirmations for Self-Love

Parents Who Bully

Choose Your Life Purposes

WHY SMART PEOPLE HURT

JOURNAL

Reflective Writing Prompts for the Smart, the Sensitive and the Creative

DR. ERIC MAISEL

BOOKS THAT SAVE LIVES

MIAMI

Published by Books That Save Lives, a division of Mango Publishing Group, Inc.

Cover Design: Elina Diaz
Cover Photo/illustration: stock.adobe.com/Dedraw Studio
Layout & Design: Elina Diaz

For permission requests, please contact the publisher at:
Mango Publishing Group
5966 South Dixie Highway, Suite 300
Miami, FL 33143
info@mango.bz

For special orders, quantity sales, course adoptions and corporate sales, please email the publisher at sales@mango.bz. For trade and wholesale sales, please contact Ingram Publisher Services at customer.service@ingramcontent.com or +1.800.509.4887.

Why Smart People Hurt Journal: Reflective Writing Prompts for the Smart, the Sensitive and the Creative

ISBN: (print) 978-1-68481-682-8
BISAC category code: SEL045000, SELF-HELP / Journaling

For Ann, 47 years into this adventure

Table of Contents

FOREWORD BY LYNDA MONK, MSW, RSW, CPCC

The *Why Smart People Hurt Journal* by Eric Maisel, PhD, offers a close look at the many things that can hurt smart, sensitive, and creative people in the first place. Things like painful family of origin experiences, workplace unfriendliness, feeling misunderstood, and having a loss of purpose in life.

The journal explores key challenges that are at the heart of why smart people might hurt, and it provides thought-provoking journal prompts to serve as openings into self-reflection, healing, growth, and new insights for the reader/journal writer.

As the leader of the International Association for Journaling Writing, I connect with journal writers from around the world every single day. These journal keepers are seekers and creatives who want to use journaling to know, grow, and care for themselves in meaningful ways. This guided *Why Smart People Hurt Journal* can help people point their journaling and self-reflection in directions that they likely would not have gone on their own.

Maisel's years as a family therapist, prolific writer, intelligent thinker, and creativity coach are evident in the wise and provocative prompts that he articulates in this journal. His life as a smart person who understands the impact of authoritarian forces, which try to silence artists and intellectuals, is felt throughout the pages of this journal.

He instills a confidence in the reader that he understands their challenges and that he can be their trusted guide into deep places within. Maisel validates readers while calling them forth to look within to alleviate some of the hurt that they might experience as smart, sensitive, and creative individuals. The self-awareness and healing for smart creatives is a benefit to individuals and the collective society alike.

There is boldness, assertiveness, and strength in the journaling prompts offered that is sure to support the reader to be brave when they reflect and write in this important and, quite likely, life-changing journal. I will highly recommend this journal to those in our IAJW journaling community and beyond. I will also benefit from using the journal myself.

This journal is good medicine for complex times like these, where smart, sensitive, and creative individuals need to be uplifted and supported to keep trusting their own inner voices on the page and in the world.

INTRODUCTION

"We humans have always used our intelligence and creativity to improve our existence, from inventing the wheel and the printing press to finding a vaccine for polio."

—Naveen Jain

We do not celebrate intelligence for its own sake. That someone is brilliant, or smarter than average, is important to humanity only because he or she may find a way to contribute to the betterment of all of us by producing a vaccine, by desalinating the sea, by opening our eyes to injustice through writing, art, or oratory, or in some other way that serves us all.

We need our best and our brightest. They do the most to keep civilization afloat. It follows that we should try to help them meet the challenges that they regularly face. That is the goal of this journal, to help you meet an array of challenges that you are likely to face or will inevitably face. I want to give you the chance to think about these pressing, poignant challenges and come up with your own best solutions.

Smart, sensitive, creative people face an array of challenges peculiar to their temperaments, outlooks, intellectual needs, psychological makeup, interpersonal realities, work opportunities, and positions in society. This journal provides you with the opportunity to consider whether any of these challenges may be confronting you—and what you might like to do to better meet them.

Not all of these challenges will pertain to you. Feel free to skip those that don't apply, but I would suggest that you give each entry some thought. The challenges discussed in those less relevant entries may in fact be pertinent, but may currently be flying under your radar. Take your time and see what thoughts and reflections arise.

This journal is a companion to my earlier book *Why Smart People Hurt*, which has been reissued under the "Books That Save Lives" imprint of Mango as *Why Smart, Creative and Highly Sensitive People Hurt*. Please take a peek there for a fuller discussion of the challenges I present in this journal. I think it will prove a welcome companion to this volume.

We might start our investigations anywhere, but let's start with your place in society. No smart person lives in a vacuum—he is part of his family, his social group, his community, his country. How will that affect him? Let's begin!

ENTRY 1

YOUR UNFRIENDLY FAMILY

A smart person, both historically and in our present times, is likely surrounded by anti-intellectualism and by people who despise artists and intellectuals. Let's begin by looking at the challenge of family antipathy to thinking critically and to creative and intellectual pursuits.

Because of the ways that very human emotions like jealousy and envy play themselves out, and because people are taught by their religions and the apparatus of their culture to follow rather than to think for themselves, a large segment of the population is antipathetic toward smart people—including mothers and fathers toward their own children and siblings toward their sisters and brothers.

Please pick one or more of the following prompts to write on and consider.

Was your family environment antipathetic to thinking and derisive of people who did a lot of thinking?

Was this antipathy aimed directly at you?

What were the consequences of this for you in childhood?

What have been the lifelong consequences of your family's attitudes?

ENTRY 2

SOCIETY AND RELIGION

Second is the challenge of religious or social opposition to critical thinking and to creative and intellectual pursuits. Religions announce, "I am the right way and the only way and follow what I say." They do not want members of their flock to think for themselves. They are therefore naturally and consistently aligned with other autocrats, like dictatorial politicians and bullying parents, who are opposed to freethinkers.

Did you grow up in a religion that demanded allegiance and rejected free thinking?

Did you passively and tacitly go along with the rules and dogmas of that religion? If so, what were the consequences of that passivity?

If you rebelled and broke with your religion or social group, what were the consequences of that rebellion?

What are the ongoing consequences of that rupture and rebellion?

ENTRY 3

WORKPLACE UNFRIENDLINESS

Third is the challenge of workplace antipathy to smartness. For example, your boss may angrily reject your suggestion for doing something in a better, smarter way because he doesn't want to upset the apple cart. A given workplace may pay lip service to an idea like innovation, but, in reality, only concerns itself with the bottom line and the status quo.

Have you found yourself in workplaces that were antipathetic to smartness?

What were the consequences for you of having to work in such an environment?

Do you currently find yourself in a workplace that is antipathetic to smartness?

How is that antipathy affecting your performance and your job satisfaction?

ENTRY 4

THE ROLE OF MASS CULTURE

A fourth, related challenge is living embedded in an anti-intellectual mass culture. Mass culture always panders to the masses—that's why it's called mass culture. If the masses want their movies to come with a happy ending, their movies will come with a happy ending. No movie director who wants his career to continue would orchestrate a certain $200,000,000 flop by opting for an unsatisfactory, true-to-life ending. Mass culture is regularly, if not always, anti-intellectual.

What do you see as the consequences for you personally of mass culture: of the advertisements you're bombarded with, of the programs television provides you with, of the movies that Hollywood makes, etc.?

What do you see as the consequences of mass culture on the people around you and the people with whom you interact?

Are you yourself obliged to play the mass culture game by virtue of the work you do, say as a screenwriter, actor, social influencer, publicist, or freelance writer?

If you wanted to reduce the influence of mass culture in your life, what might you do or change?

ENTRY 5

THE BIGGER PICTURE

Fifth is the challenge of living in a society that feels threatened by, and despises, its artists and intellectuals. It is a hallmark of fascism, and of the conservative and authoritarian forces in every society, to target artists and intellectuals, as those are the people most likely to speak out against oppression and injustice and most likely to rebel against totalitarianism.

In what sense or senses do you experience your society as against you?

Have there been concrete instances of this antipathy?

What have been the personal consequences, if any, of this antipathy?

Do you think that there might be another society that suits you better? If so, do you have any thoughts about switching or any plans for switching?

ENTRY 6

FEELING DIFFERENT

For the reasons we just discussed, and for many other reasons as well, smart, sensitive, creative folks regularly experience, and find themselves confronted by, five specific feelings: they feel different, they feel misunderstood, they feel underutilized, they feel alienated, and they feel special, but also small. Let's look at these five in turn.

Just as a very short or a very tall person is likely to feel different from those around him, just as a Jew is likely to feel out of place in a mosque and a Muslim is likely to feel out of place in a synagogue, just as an African-American golfer is going to experience herself as an object of scrutiny (and maybe ridicule and scorn) at an all-white country club, so a smart person is likely to feel different as he navigates life.

Have you experienced the feeling that you are different from other people?

Does this feeling translate as "better than other people"? Is this feeling of difference actually a feeling of superiority?

What have been the consequences of feeling different?

Would you like to feel "more like other people" or are you content feeling yourself different?

ENTRY 7

FEELING MISUNDERSTOOD

Smart people regularly feel misunderstood. For example, if you are ahead of the curve on some idea—let's say, evolution—and people shake their heads and claim that you are anti-religion and the devil incarnate, aren't you going to feel misunderstood? Maybe you aren't anti-religion or an atheist at all—but can you possibly make people understand that, given how angry and inflamed they're feeling?

Do you regularly feel misunderstood?

To what do you attribute that feeling? That others simply don't "get you" or your ideas? Or is something else going on?

What, if any, have been the consequences of feeling misunderstood?

What, if any, have been the consequences of actually being misunderstood?

ENTRY 8

FEELING UNDERUTILIZED

Then there's the challenge of feeling underutilized. Many, if not most, smart people end up doing routine work that does not make any real use of their smarts. As an estate attorney, they may provide the same sort of advice over and over again; as a painter, they may be obliged to produce their signature work, even if that work bores them; as an entrepreneur, they may spend days fulfilling orders and putting out fires and not really thinking about anything.

Does your work, occupation, day job, or career make use of enough of you?

____

____

____

____

____

If it doesn't, have you been able to find other ways to utilize yourself more fully or other outlets for your natural talents and gifts?

What, if any, have been the consequences of your limited ability to fully utilize yourself?

What new efforts might you make to utilize yourself more?

ENTRY 9

FEELING ALIENATED

A fourth challenge is feeling alienated. If you experience the people around you as antipathetic to thinking, if you find their conversations banal and their concerns superficial, if you see them more as threats than as allies, and if you "see through" to the void and understand the unreality of their myth-making (say, for example, about Heaven or Nirvana), the feeling that all of that engenders is likely to be one of alienation.

Do you feel alienated from other people? Can you identify why?

Do you have trouble in social situations engaging in everyday conversation and/or cocktail party banter?

Which do you find more alienating, the superficiality of most people or the irrationality of their belief systems?

Would you like to feel less alienated, are you resigned to feeling alienated, or are you even quite comfortable feeling alienated?

ENTRY 10

FEELING SPECIAL... AND SMALL

Then there's the odd but real challenge of feeling special but also small. A contemporary smart person is likely to feel two contradictory feelings, first, that, by virtue of his intelligence, he is special, and, second, that despite that intelligence and its specialness, he is still just a mere mortal susceptible to toothaches, betrayals, pratfalls, and every other exigency of life.

Have you experienced these contradictory feelings, of feeling special *and* feeling puny and all-too-human?

How have these contradictory feelings played themselves out? By, for example, embarking on a large project and then feeling not at all equal to tackling it or completing it? Or in some other way?

Do you see this dynamic in play in the lives of the smart people you know? What have you seen?

What are your headline thoughts about the five feelings we discussed in the last five entries?

ENTRY 11

STUCK ON THE DULL TRACK

You may feel small for another set of reasons as well, having to do with having been relegated to the dull track. Families and sometimes whole societies decide that this child is worth educating and that one isn't, that this child is naturally smart and that this child is naturally dull, that this one should work with his brain and that that one should work with his hands, decisions often made on the basis of class or caste. Many very bright children, pigeonholed early, end up in the dull category or in the not-worth-educating category, with lifelong negative consequences.

Were you pigeonholed early in a nonintellectual direction?

If so, what were the consequences of that pigeonholing?

Have you been able to find satisfactory outlets for your native intelligence?

Might you still be able to find satisfactory outlets for your native intelligence?

ENTRY 12

AIMED IN THE DIRECTION OF "SAFETY"

A related challenge is being pushed and aimed in a "safe" direction. For example, a child may be pushed in the direction of what seems like a safely attainable goal, like, for instance, elementary school teaching, and discouraged from imagining that she might be a college professor, which may seem too lofty and unattainable.

Were you advised to play it safe and not "dream above your station"?

If so, what were the consequences of that advice?

Is it still possible to attain the position you crave?

If so, what might be the steps to take to move in that direction?

ENTRY 13

THE FAMILY BUSINESS

A variation on this theme is having been aimed toward the family business. For example, a child's parents may run a restaurant or a dry-cleaning business and fully expect all the children in the family to join the family business, irrespective of their individual desires or abilities.

Were you told that you were obliged to join the family business?

Did you agree to that? If so, what were the consequences?

Did you disagree and rebel? If so, what were the consequences?

If you are currently "trapped" in the family business, can you envision an exit strategy?

ENTRY 14

HOW SOCIAL PIGEONHOLING WORKS

Related is the challenge of social pigeonholing. For example, you may grow up in a society where girls are not educated and are expected to become wives and mothers or, if they are allowed to work, to rise no "higher" than teacher or nurse.

Were you born into an anti-intellectual religion or society that saw schooling and thinking as dangerous?

Were you born into a social group where intellectual work was ridiculed?

Were you born into a society that devalued thinking in general or that devalued it for certain segments of society?

If any of the above were true for you, what have been the consequences?

ENTRY 15

HIDING YOUR LIGHT UNDER A BUSHEL

Maybe the sort of pigeonholing I've been describing occurred because you never really showed off your smarts? Maybe your challenge was a lack of confidence or the habit of hiding your light under a bushel? For example, a given smart child may look dull because she doesn't feel confident expressing herself or doesn't feel particularly safe expressing herself, and as a result is presumed to be not particularly bright.

Were you considered not particularly bright because you hid your brightness?

What were the consequences of you hiding your intelligence under a bushel?

____

____

____

____

____

____

Do you still hide your native intelligence under a bushel?

____

____

____

____

____

____

____

If so, what steps might you take to remedy that?

ENTRY 16

THE DAY JOB PROBLEM

Let's say that you survived your society's selection process and were able to pursue your intellectual or artistic interests. This leads naturally to two different sets of problems, one having to do with your chosen path not paying the bills and the second having to do with your chosen path indeed paying the bills—but with some important caveats. Let's begin with the first scenario.

Say that you're a novelist whose writing career isn't paying the bills. That means that you will need "other work"—and most "other work" is not intellectually interesting. This can be especially true of a day job: a job meant to pay the rent while you pursue something personally meaningful like acting, painting, or writing. A dullard with a trust fund does not need a day job, but a genius may well.

Do you find yourself in the position of needing a day job?

Is that your best option? Or are there perhaps other options?

To what extent do you resent the fact that you're obliged to "waste all that time" working a day job?

What is your vision for the future? Do you see yourself as working a day job for a short amount of time, an indeterminate amount of time, or "forever"?

ENTRY 17

YOUR REMAINING NEURONS

A related challenge is the challenge of managing to do real intellectual work while holding down a day job. Say that you find a typical day job, one that ends up taxing you and consuming more of your day than you thought it would. How likely is it that you will find yourself rushing home, eager and alert enough to work on your novel?

Typical day jobs, like waiting tables and bartending, or their contemporary online equivalents, may prove at once taxing and dull—the worst of both worlds. You may have been thinking that, since a day job isn't intellectually taxing, you will save neurons for your real thinking work—but is that plan working out?

If your plan was to work a day job *and* get your real work done, have you found that a viable plan?

What has been the hardest part of making that plan work? Physical exhaustion? Mental exhaustion? The sheer number of hours consumed by the job? Or something else?

What might you try so as to make this plan work better?

Is it time for a different plan?

ENTRY 18

TOO LONG AT THE DAY JOB

Maybe the day job plan can work for some number of years—but can it work indefinitely? Won't it grow very old? Maybe you found a decent day job and it served your needs well enough. But can it still serve your needs—psychologically, existentially, and practically—after two years, after five years, after ten years? Or will the reality of it become less and less bearable?

Have you been at your current day job for a significant amount of time?

Is it becoming harder and harder to go to work? Are you calling in sick more, coming in late, leaving early, doing a less-than-stellar job, or in some other way acting out your fatigue and resentment?

Are there any changes you can make to your current situation to make your day job more tolerable?

If it is time to leave—or past time—what might the next plan be?

ENTRY 19

THE SECOND CAREER PROBLEM

Finding a day job is one typical response to the problem of our intellectual or artistic work not paying the bills. Pursuing a second career is another typical response. A smart, sensitive, creative person may decide to pursue a career not likely to make her much money—let's say, writing poetry—and then come to the conclusion that maybe the best way to pay the bills is to pursue a second career, something reasonably interesting in its own right and likely to pay the bills—let's say, a second career like law or psychotherapy. How well is that likely to work?

Have you chosen a second career to complement and supplement your main creative or intellectual work?

Have you found that second career more taxing and consuming than you thought it would be? If you don't have a second career, what would that look like for you?

What have you found most surprising about launching that second career?

____

____

____

____

____

____

____

Are there some changes you might institute that would make your second career plan more viable?

____

____

____

____

____

____

ENTRY 20

SURPRISING SHORTFALLS

It may prove surprising and disheartening to discover that your second career, chosen for its viability and financial stability, is much less viable and stable than you had supposed it would be. Maybe it is very hard getting clients or customers; maybe even a full roster of clients or customers, after the office rent and all the other expenses are paid, does not amount to a full living. How disappointing!

Has your second career proven as financially viable as you thought it would prove?

Has it proven as stable as you thought it would prove?

Is there a way to have it produce more income, short of working more hours?

Is there a way to stabilize it and make it less of a rollercoaster ride?

ENTRY 21

SHEER OVERWHELM

Maybe your efforts at juggling a second career, an intellectual or creative pursuit, and everything else in life have reached greater crisis proportions than chaos and disorganization. Maybe they have reached the place of sheer and complete overwhelm. Are you there?

Are you in a state of constant overwhelm?

What do you experience as the psychological consequences of that overwhelm?

______

______

______

______

______

______

What do you experience as the physical consequences of that overwhelm?

______

______

______

______

______

______

Can you see a way to create a less overwhelming life?

ENTRY 22

TRAPPED IN SMALLNESS

Maybe you've landed on intellectual work that actually pays the bills, say as a tenured college professor. What a blessing! But that isn't the end of the story.

In ancient Greece, a thinker or an artist could be as wide-ranging as they wanted to be, doing science, art, philosophy, and whatever else excited or interested them. An Aristotle, Plato, Socrates, Democritus, Pythagoras, or other Greek thinker could engage in what was called "natural philosophy"—that is, they could take an interest in anything and everything.

Nowadays that is rarely true. We have arrived at an age of narrow specialization and, with it, serious repercussions. For example, your academic research may have led you, pretty much inevitably, to a very narrow, restrictive, and constrictive place. Maybe you are a biologist who has landed in the narrow place of learning more and more about just one cellular process. That's what happens!

Have you been painted into a corner, intellectually speaking?

Visualize yourself escaping from that corner. What do you see?

Describe one tactic or strategy that might help you break free of your current situation.

____

____

____

____

____

____

Are there any people to enlist or resources to employ to help you escape that corner?

____

____

____

____

____

____

ENTRY 23

THE UNINTERESTING DAY-TO-DAY

A second challenge is discovering that your biggest and best ideas clash with your day-to-day activities. For example, maybe you are a lawyer who is deeply interested in the big ideas of intellectual property law, but you find yourself spending your days litigating small, murky intellectual property disputes.

Do your day-to-day activities rob you of the chance to think about the big ideas in your field?

Do you see a way to at least partially pursue those big ideas?

Pick a big idea from your field that interests you. Visualize yourself pursuing it. What do you see?

Is there a way to maneuver yourself in your field so that you get to entertain big ideas more often?

ENTRY 24

STANDARD THINKING

A related challenge is that your field has "hardened" into a standardized way of thinking, and now there is no room for innovation. For example, maybe you are a physicist who can only garner research money for yet another study that supports the standard model. What if you want to go in a radically new direction, and no one will fund your research?

Are you working in a field that has "hardened" in this way?

What have been the consequences of that hardening for the field?

What have been the consequences of that hardening for you personally?

What solutions or part-solutions seem possible?

ENTRY 25

STICK TO THAT, PLEASE!

Say that you're a writer who would love to be a generalist and write about whatever interests you. But editors are pushing back and indicating that they want you to stick to the one thing for which you are best known and for which you have the largest following. What will you do?

Do you see a way to balance writing what you want to write with writing what they want you to write?

Given that self-publishing is always an option, what are your thoughts on focusing on self-publishing, so as to be able to write whatever you want to write?

When the marketplace demands that you stick to one thing, what strategies might you employ to maintain and explore your other interests?

Have you had the experience of being told to stick to one thing? How did you react?

ENTRY 26

NOTHING OF INTEREST

A rather different sort of problem from the preceding ones is also possible—and even likely. In the preceding examples, I pictured you having chosen a pursuit like novel-writing, criminal law, or astrophysics. You followed some interest, an interest that may even have amounted to a passion. But what if nothing has ever really interested you? Or, along the same lines, what if things have only momentarily interested you and amounted to passing fancies? What a difficult and painful way to live, to be smart and creative but not have any outlets or passions! Is this you?

Has nothing ever really interested you, intellectually or artistically speaking?

If so, do you have a sense of why this might be true?

What might you try to do in order to "generate some interest" in a field, a medium, an idea, etc.?

Picture yourself "really interested" in something. What do you see?

ENTRY 27

INTEREST...BUT NO PASSION

A different but related challenge is having lots of interests but not feeling particularly passionate about any of them. Maybe you take a momentary interest in something, like painting or screenwriting, but your interest never moves past amusement to something stronger. You might frame this as "I love so many things, I don't know what to choose" or "I'm so easily distracted" or you might frame it in some other way—but the bottom line is that all of your interests turn dull, sometimes within moments of announcing it.

Do you have lots of interests that stop interesting you almost immediately?

____

____

____

____

____

Do you have a sense of why that happens?

Do you see a way to keep an interest interesting and/or to turn it into a passion?

Where would you say "interest" comes from? What are its sources, do you think?

ENTRY 28

PASSION...BUT NO PASSION PROJECT

Maybe you love something dearly—let's say, fiction. You know you love it, you've always loved, you still love it. But you've never been able to start that novel you've always dreamed of penning. You have all the passion a person could need, but something is preventing you from unleashing that passion on a real, specific project. What's going on?

Are you passionate about something but unable or unwilling to unleash that passion on a specific passion project?

Is it that you are more unable or more unwilling? Or does the problem lie elsewhere?

Can you name a passion project that you might embark upon if only you weren't reluctant or resistant?

Picture yourself working on a passion project. What do you see?

ENTRY 29

PASSION PROJECT RESISTANCE

Maybe yours is the following situation. You are clear about your passion project—let's say, writing your memoir. But you rarely get to it and feel significantly resistant to working on it. You're certain that the project is important to you and fairly certain that it might be of interest to others, but still "something" (or more than one "something") is keeping you from working regularly—or even much at all. Is this your situation?

Do you have a passion project that you rarely work on?

____

____

____

____

Do you have some ideas about what may be generating your reluctance or resistance?

What might you try in order to reduce that reluctance and overcome that resistance?

Picture yourself working daily on your passion project. What do you see?

ENTRY 30

INNER NOISE AND MONKEY MIND

So far, we've looked at external challenges, stressors like an anti-intellectual culture, difficulties making a living, getting caught in a small corner of a field, etc. Now, let's begin to look at what's inside: at a smart person's inner world. We'll begin by examining how inner noise can prevent us from doing our best thinking. According to research, people have on average 60,000 thoughts a day. That's no problem—unless those thoughts pester us and produce the experience of what Buddhists call "monkey mind." Is that a challenge for you?

Do you have the sense that too much inner noise is preventing you from doing your best thinking?

Are there certain thoughts that are "noisiest" and that have risen to the pestering level of negative obsession?

What do you do to quiet that inner noise? Do you have some tactics that work?

What would you like to try as a new tactic for quieting that inner noise?

ENTRY 31

UNDERESTIMATING YOUR SMARTS

A related challenge, and a poignant one, is misunderstanding or underestimating your native intelligence if, all your life, your inner environment has been extremely noisy. You may have long thought that you aren't smart enough to tackle some intellectual pursuit or other—but what if that's a miscalculation or a misunderstanding and not the fact of the matter? Maybe all that pestering noise has prevented you from manifesting your intellectual or artistic potential—something that happens all the time.

Do you think that it's possible that you've underestimated your native intelligence because your noisy mind has stopped you from doing your best thinking?

If you believe that you may have underestimated how smart you are, what were the consequences of that underestimation?

What experiment might you run to test if you have or haven't underestimated your native smarts?

What tactics do you use to reduce monkey mind?

ENTRY 32

BEING TOO VIGILANT

If you haven't felt particularly safe in life, that can easily produce a cautionary over-vigilance that can reduce your ability to think. When your mind is fixed on one particular thought—say, the pestering concern whether the novel you've sent around to literary agents will be accepted or rejected—it is very hard to do any new or deep thinking. Your neurons, having gathered together to vigilantly await the outcome of the query process, are hardly available to work on your next project, are they?

Are you regularly over-vigilant, and do you pay too much attention to a given thought?

Can you identify one of those thoughts? What seems to hook you to that thought and hold your attention there?

What can you do to unhook and release thoughts to which you are paying too much attention?

If nothing has worked particularly well so far, what new tactic or strategy might you try?

ENTRY 33

FEELING UNSAFE

Feeling unsafe reduces our ability to think. If enemy missiles are raining down on your neighborhood, it is going to prove very hard, maybe verging on impossible, to do any quality thinking. That is an extreme example—but there are countless everyday examples, from not feeling safe in your neighborhood when you go out to shop to not feeling safe in your own home because of a bullying parent or mate.

Do you feel safe in your general environment? Safe enough to think?

What about your work environment? Do you feel safe there, or do you feel scrutinized, judged, micro-managed, or otherwise inhibited and unsafe?

What about your family environment? Are family conflicts producing inner turmoil and making you feel unsafe in your own home?

What about your own thoughts? Do your own thoughts feel safe or unsafe to think?

ENTRY 34

WHEN ANXIETY STRIKES

Anxiety conspires to produce noise and reduce our ability to think. Anxiety is an early warning system against danger and can sometimes arise at the right moment (to warn us against a real threat) or at the wrong moment (to prevent us from performing well or taking a necessary risk), and it can pester smart people more than they realize. Is anxiety a challenge for you?

Anxiety is a great silencer. Do you experience it as silencing you and keeping you from doing your best thinking?

How does anxiety manifest in your life? As mental confusion? Physically, as headaches or nausea? As fatigue? Or in some other way?

What do you know to do to manage or reduce your experience of anxiety?

Is there something new you'd like to try to manage or reduce your experience of anxiety?

ENTRY 35

YOUR TANGLED THINKING

Thinking can be a tangled affair and, if our thinking is particularly tangled, that will inevitably get in the way of our ability to do intellectual or creative work. A given thought may arise for all sorts of reasons, producing the feeling that you can't really trust it or that you don't really understand it. A simple-sounding thought like "I'm tired" may really mean, "I'm sad, I can't face the work that I have to do, and I think I want some Scotch." That's a lot of entanglement!

Do you have the sense that many of your thoughts arise for less than obvious reasons and therefore can't be taken at face value?

Would you like to better understand what such tangled thoughts "mean" and where they come from?

____

____

____

____

____

____

Is there a particular thought that you regularly think that you know is tangled and in need of some unknotting?

____

____

____

____

____

Picture yourself unknotting that particular thought. Unknot it bit by bit. Then journal on that experience.

ENTRY 36

UNWANTED OBSESSIONS

Not every obsession is unwanted. Maybe you're obsessing about a plot point in the screenplay that you're writing. That may be exactly what you need to be doing. But unwanted obsessions usually far outnumber our productive ones.

Is there one unwanted thought (or one sort of unwanted thought) that you keep obsessing about that you would prefer to stop thinking about?

The next time you think that unwanted thought, what might you decide to think instead? (This is called "thought replacement" or "thought substitution.")

If you have some way of noticing that the unwanted thought is "coming," what might you try to do to stop it from arising at all? (This is called "thought blocking.")

Can you distinguish between your productive obsessions and your unwanted obsessions? What distinguishes the two?

ENTRY 37

A RAIN OF THOUGHTS

If you have an active brain, your brain will busily keep producing thoughts (full thoughts, half-thoughts, fragments of thoughts, etc.) whether or not you really want them and even if you are trying to think about something else. How can you solve that knotty physics problem if you're caught in a thunderstorm of other thoughts?

Do you experience your inner life as a "rain of thoughts"?

Do lots of unwanted, inconsequential, and incidental thoughts intrude on your consciousness as you are trying to think about something else (like learning some new bit of technology)?

What do you think might help you "turn off that faucet"?

Imagine that your rain of thoughts stopped. Would you experience peace and quiet? Or would you feel bereft as if you had lost something?

ENTRY 38

REPETITIVE THOUGHTS

Often, as we are thinking about something, our minds default to the most usual or customary answers. For example, you may be trying to promote the novel you've just written, and your mind keeps returning you to the idea that you should be posting regularly on Instagram. That "Instagram thought" keeps repeating itself, preventing you from percolating up some other, new ideas. Do you find this happening a lot?

Can you identify a certain thought or a certain sort of thought that you know falls into this category of repetitive thinking?

____

____

____

____

____

Why do you suppose it keeps repeating itself? What is that repetition serving?

How might you keep repetitive thoughts from repeating themselves? Do some ideas, tactics, or strategies pop to mind?

Picture a repetitive thought repeating itself. What sort of conversation might you have with it—or with yourself—at that moment?

ENTRY 39

LOST THOUGHTS

A smart, creative, sensitive person is often a busy person with little time available to examine, capture, or even really notice all the thoughts that are arising, including those very good ones that amount to her best ideas and best solutions. Consequently, those best ideas and solutions just pass on by, amounting to a real intellectual loss.

Do you often have good ideas that immediately vanish because you aren't in the habit of really noticing them or capturing them as they rush on by?

What might help you notice them, at least long enough to know whether you want to examine them and/or save them?

____

____

____

____

____

____

How might you save them, given that they might come at any time of the day or night, including when you're in the middle of something else? Might you use a small notebook? An app on your phone? Or something else?

____

____

____

____

Having saved them, what might you "do" with them?

ENTRY 40

THOUGHT INVESTIGATION

A smart person's stock-in-trade is thinking. But he may prove no better than the next person when it comes to investigating his own thoughts to see if they ought to be countenanced. Not every thought ought to be respected, because a given thought may have arisen from some defensive place, some mischievous place, or some other shadowy place.

It would be good to interrogate thoughts as if they were suspects in a criminal case. This might sound like, "Okay, thought, what's going on? What are you doing in my head? Are you serving me? Are you out for some mischief? What exactly are you doing?" Say that you pass by the window of a pastry shop. A gorgeous cake catches your eye. You hear yourself say, "That cake looks delicious." Are you alerted to the fact that maybe that's a suspect thought, maybe having to do with your desire to jettison your diet? Wouldn't it be good to know that?

Are you in the habit of wondering if a given thought might be suspect or not?

If that wonder does cross your mind, what do you do next? Do you actually do a little investigating?

Can you recall a time when it really paid dividends to not accept a thought at face value but to investigate it instead?

What thought have you had today (or recently) that might be worth investigating and "interrogating"?

ENTRY 41

DEFENSIVE NOT KNOWING

What can get in the way of successfully investigating our own thoughts is our defensiveness. A smart person is just as defensive as the next person. How can we successfully interrogate our thoughts if we've erected a wall of denial and don't really want to know what our thoughts are signifying or hiding? Given that this is an all-too-human reaction to our own dangerous-feeling thoughts, what might help us reduce that defensiveness so that we are freer to know what's really going on?

Picture a wall between you and your secrets, the secrets you keep from yourself. How might you go about taking that wall down?

Picture a few bricks in that wall being removed. Take a peek. What do you see on the other side?

Does it feel safe to remove a few more bricks? Are you willing to learn more?

What about removing the whole wall? What might the consequences be of such an amazing, dramatic, brave act?

ENTRY 42

NO COMMENT

A given suspect thought that you are interrogating may simply "refuse to talk." On the advice of counsel—on the advice of some protective mechanism somewhere deep inside of you—your suspect thought may simply reply, "No comment." What then?

If you have the feeling that a thought that you're thinking may be suspect, but you can't figure out whether or not it really is, what might you do?

Is there a particular suspect thought, maybe a repetitive one, that you would like to interrogate? How might you proceed?

Imagine a suspect thought "opening up" to you. What might you learn?

What is your go-to or favorite defense mechanism? Do you know?

ENTRY 43

GETTING A GRIP

We've looked at your inner world, your cognitive style, and your possible cognitive challenges from many angles: with regard to inner noise, over-vigilance, obsessive thinking, tangled thinking, suspect thoughts, and more. This all comes under the heading of getting a clearer understanding of how your thoughts operate and meeting the challenges connected with the Buddha's admonition that we "get a grip on our mind." That is a huge challenge!

What might the habit of investigating your own thoughts look like? Would you like to create a plan or a system?

Journal to the prompt, "I think that I would like to learn more about how my inner language works. To that end, I will do the following."

Create an "I will try to only think thoughts that serve me" affirmation...and try it out.

Picture yourself as a "cognitive detective." Create a story where you break the case and, by so doing, improve your cognitive landscape.

ENTRY 44

TOLERATING PROCESS

Some challenges can't be eliminated. Rather, a smart, sensitive, creative person must simply make peace with them. These include the realities of process, the likely presence of some amount of sadness and anxiety, the obligation to tolerate solitude (and the loneliness that may come with that), etc. Let's look at several of these.

Smart people often find themselves disappointed and troubled by the realities of process, including the reality of mistakes, messes, pratfalls, and everything else that process entrails. This might sound like, "If I'm so smart, why can't I figure this out?" Why can't you figure it out? Likely because the solution hasn't come to you yet...

Do you leave creative or intellectual projects incomplete because you find the realities of process, like ideas morphing and motivation flagging, too taxing?

Are you comfortable with the idea that a lot of your ideas and creative efforts will prove only ordinary? Or do you need everything you do to be brilliant or perfect?

The creative and thinking processes both come with mistakes and messes. Do you find mistakes easy or hard to deal with? Do they tend to derail you?

What part of your relationship with process would you like to improve?

ENTRY 45

THE REALITY OF CIRCUMSTANCES

What if your circumstances are far from ideal and make thinking or creating hard? What if, for example, you live in a noisy environment with lots of roommates or lots of siblings and loads of dramas and squabbles? How easy will your best thinking be to come by in such circumstances? Can you make peace with the idea that you must think and create right in the middle of your current circumstances?

Are your circumstances getting in the way of your ability to think or create?

Is there something about those circumstances that you can change?

If those circumstances can't be changed, can you make peace with that reality and find ways to still think and create?

In your mind's eye, picture the "perfect circumstances" for thinking and creating. What do you see?

ENTRY 46

TOLERATING SOLITUDE

Many smart people are deeply uncomfortable being with themselves quietly and quickly flee the experience of solitude, as if solitude somehow constituted a danger. Some even find solitude a near-death experience and see quiet as a portal to the void. If this is you, how much thinking or creating can possibly get done? Can you make peace with the fact that you are obliged to tolerate solitude, if you have any hope of getting your creative or intellectual work done?

Do you tend to hate solitude and flee it, or does it not bother you?

Why do you think that is so? What do you think may be going on?

What might you try so as to make solitude more tolerable?

Can you make peace with the idea that solitude is necessary?

ENTRY 47

THE DANGERS OF SOLITUDE

On the flip side, you may tolerate solitude beautifully and experience it as your preferred way of being: alone with yourself thinking, reading, creating, dreaming, musing, and so on. With that comes its own set of dangers and consequences, including relationship difficulties, loneliness, and general alienation. Are you too comfortable with solitude? Can you make peace with the idea that there is more to life than a happy solitude?

What do you love most about your solitude?

____

____

____

____

____

____

Does your natural desire for solitude bring with it too much isolation and loneliness?

Do you sometimes feels alienated from your fellow human beings?

Would you like to feel more connected to other people, or are you fine as you are?

ENTRY 48

INSATIABILITY

Brain power, the creative impulse, and massive life energy combine to create a kind of insatiable hunger, in which, as soon as something is completed, the hunger to rush on to that next delicious, tempting project produces new pressure, giving life a relentless coloration. Is this your experience of life?

Do you find yourself always hungry?

Do you experience this hunger as a kind of relentless pressure?

If you are always hungry, what might you do to feel more satisfied "in the moment" and less pressed to rush on to the next project, thrill, or conquest?

What do you see as the dangers of insatiability and of this constant hunger?

ENTRY 49

COMPETITION

Smart, creative individuals often choose careers that are highly competitive in nature. Whether it's in law, fine arts, academia, novel-writing, business, or some other competitive sphere, supply outweighs demand, and only a percentage of the folks engaged in those professions will succeed. Are you at ease with the idea that you are competing and that maybe you must compete?

Is your profession necessarily and naturally competitive? Have you reconciled yourself to that reality?

Have you found a way to "not compete" that is working for you?

How has this built-in competitiveness played itself out in your life?

Would you like to become "more competitive," for the sake of succeeding? What would that look like?

ENTRY 50

THE SMART GAP

Another poignant challenge is realizing that you are short on the intelligence required to do something at a high level—say, abstract mathematics—and that therefore you are consigned to either do something else or to continue along at a lower level than you crave. How can a person make peace with this "smart gap," which is so intrinsically and fundamentally painful?

Is what you are experiencing really a smart gap or a consequence of high anxiety, your circumstances, some intellectually laziness, or something else?

If this smart gap is about something else, what does that suggest? That maybe there is a way to "close" that smart gap, through anxiety management, changed circumstances, etc.?

If you can't see a way to close that smart gap, how will you proceed?

What would allow you to access more of your native intelligence?

ENTRY 51

INEVITABLE SADNESS

There is a natural connection between intelligence and sadness. If you have a mind that refuses to accept easy answers to hard questions and that sees through much conventional wisdom and the blandishments of a consumer society, isn't some sadness bound to follow?

If you had a scientific bent and a clear understanding of the political and environmental perils facing our world, wouldn't you find yourself in some rather significant despair? Aren't you going to have to make peace with a certain amount of sadness?

Is sadness a chronic issue for you?

____

____

____

____

____

What do you see as its sources?

How does it manifest? As fatigue? As a lack of motivation? In other ways?

How might you use your creativity and your native intelligence to help reduce your experience of sadness?

ENTRY 52

INEVITABLE ANXIETY

We've chatted about anxiety already. It's worth chatting about again. If your smartness, sensitivity, and creativity propel you in the direction of, say, writing screenplays, won't you experience more-than-usual anxiety by virtue of how hard it is to make it as a screenwriter? If the creative process involves constant choosing, won't all that choosing provoke anxiety? If your excellent ideas must be defended in the marketplace of ideas, won't that public performance generate a measure of anxiety? Aren't there countless reasons why a smart person will be obliged to make peace with a significant amount of inevitable anxiety?

What, in your view, might be the connection or connections between intelligence and anxiety?

Are you susceptible to high anxiety? Do you have a sense of why that might be?

How might you employ your intelligence to help you reduce or manage the heightened anxiety that comes your way?

Can you make peace with the idea that anxiety might prove your lifelong companion?

ENTRY 53

ADDICTION RISKS

There is also a natural connection between intelligence and addiction. When you have a mind that wants to "grab," that grabbing might involve ideas or it might involve cravings. If you happen to have been born with a lot of life energy, passion, smarts, individuality, and a bursting creative nature, isn't that the exact equivalent of having a very large appetite—and isn't a large appetite itself a risk factor for addiction?

What do you see as the connection, if any, between intelligence and addiction?

What do you see as the connection, if any, between creativity and addiction?

What do you see as the connection, if any, between sensitivity and addiction?

Are addictive tendencies challenges for you? If they are, how might you handle them better?

ENTRY 54

DISTRACTIBILITY

If your brain is firing on all cylinders and providing you with lots of ideas, and if you enjoy your own ideas, won't each new interesting idea distract you from the previous one, making concentration difficult? Won't doing boring work prove difficult? Aren't you going to have to make peace with a certain level of distractibility?

What do you see as the connection between intelligence and distractibility?

Are you susceptible to distractibility? Do you have the sense that you are more susceptible to distractibility than the next person?

Is this distractibility something more to make peace with or to challenge?

If you wanted to challenge or reduce your distractibility, what might you try?

ENTRY 55

THE STORY OF ENERGY

A smart, sensitive, creative person must learn how to tolerate states and conditions that are not necessarily easy to tolerate, like runaway energy. A smart person is likely to find herself in a highly complicated relationship with her own energy supply.

This is an underexplored area, rarely discussed in mainstream Western psychology, philosophy, or medicine, but one that is likely of great importance to you. What, for instance, if it's the case that you came into the world with a ton of life energy at your disposal, a ton of what the Chinese call chi, your life force. How will that reality play itself out?

If you came into the world bursting with energy—curious, energetic, speedy, etc.—how has having "all that energy" played itself out in your life?

____

____

____

____

____

____

What do you see as the potential connection between being born with a lot of energy and ending up with label or "diagnosis" of ADHD, ADD, etc.?

____

____

____

____

____

____

How do you "use all that energy"? Do you use that energy in ways that work for you? Or does all that energy actually harm you?

____

____

____

____

____

____

Has that energy remained constant over time? Has it increased or decreased?

____

____

____

____

____

____

ENTRY 56

IN SHORT SUPPLY

What if you have the opposite problem, that, instead of coming into the world with so much energy that it needs constant attention and management, you came into the world short on energy; now you find yourself without enough life force to sustain your intellectual or creative pursuits and the life you know you want to live? What then?

Do you have the sense that you came into the world with insufficient energy? What are your reasons for thinking that?

Imagine that you could "increase your energy supply." How might you go about doing that?

If you in fact have a limited amount of energy, how will you best apportion it?

If you suffer from the thing called "depression," might that actually be more of a low energy state than a mood disorder?

ENTRY 57

ENERGY SUPPRESSION

Maybe you were born with all the energy you needed to live a creative, intellectual life, but you bottled that energy up because it wasn't safe to express it or expend it in the household into which you were born? And maybe you've mistaken suppressed high energy for low energy? That regularly happens!

In childhood, were you made to feel like your natural energy was a problem, something that the people around you wanted "to go away"?

Do you feel that over time you began to suppress your natural energy?

If so, what have been the consequences of all that suppression?

Would you like to release or recover that energy? What might that look like?

ENTRY 58

RACING DOWN THE TRACKS

Our energy can get the better of us and send us racing in dangerous and uncontrolled directions, toward the thing called "mania," toward an addiction, or toward unwanted behaviors meant to alleviate all that pressure as we pass the time frantically. Energy accelerates us—but then we can find ourselves racing uncontrollably, like a train with the accelerator stuck and the brakeman out to lunch.

Does your energy sometimes seem "out of control"?

What does that look like? If we observed you, what would we see you doing and how would we see you acting?

What might help you better "put the brakes" on that racing energy? Do you have some healthy methods or tactics that work?

Can you distinguish between racing energy that affects the mind and racing energy that affects the body?

ENTRY 59

ROLLERCOASTER ENERGY

Maybe we possess a lot of energy, even "too much" energy. Then we expend it in some way—and then feel drained and depleted. Isn't this a cycle that mimics bipolar disorder and that is going to be experienced as a certain sort of psychological and physical rollercoaster ride? Energy bursting, energy depleted, energy bursting, energy depleted—is this a familiar picture?

Picture yourself working very hard at something, either physically or mentally. Wouldn't that naturally deplete your energy?

Likewise, wouldn't your natural energy return after a time, after it's been depleted? Wouldn't you begin to feel "energetic" again?

Do you think these two states together, energy depletion and energy replenishment, functionally look like a rollercoaster ride of ups and downs? Why or why not?

What might you do to better deal with those ups and downs and those highs and lows?

ENTRY 60

SITTING ON A HIGH HORSE

Just as a tall person can lord it over shorter people without really noticing what he or she is doing, a smart person can act special and incline in the direction of arrogance, grandiosity, and narcissism just by virtue of being smart or believing himself to be smart. This might sound internally like "I'm surrounded by such fools!" or "People are such gullible idiots!"

Over the next several entries, we'll look at this particular challenge: that you may have gotten on a high horse, causing all sorts of relationship difficulties. To begin with, maybe you regularly dismiss and reject the ideas of a loved one because you've consciously or unconsciously labeled him or her as "just not that bright." In the process, you've angered and alienated that person. That won't work very well!

Do you wave off the opinions of people you consider not as bright as you, including family members and other loved ones? Can you think of a recent example?

Are you aware whether that behavior has alienated or angered the people you've dismissed that way?

Has this dynamic contributed to relationship difficulties in the past?

Is this dynamic contributing to relationship difficulties in the present?

ENTRY 61

I AM SO SPECIAL!

A related challenge is feeling too special to actually do the work. For example, an arrogant writer may presume that his rough first draft is all the work he has to do and that "someone else" (maybe a publisher privileged to purchase this great work) should polish it for him; everyone should be able to see its brilliance, even if it is only a rough first draft.

Do you never quite finish things because doing the work required to finish things is "beneath your dignity"?

Do you claim to be a "big ideas" person for whom the details are too petty and too boring to bother with?

____

____

____

____

____

____

Have you been regularly told that you should "grow up" and finish things?

____

____

____

____

____

____

If this is you, are you interested in changing this dynamic and beginning to do all the work necessary in order to satisfactorily complete things?

ENTRY 62

A SENSE OF ENTITLEMENT

A related challenge is a sense of entitlement leading to serious mischief. For example, in Dostoevsky's *Crime and Punishment*, the main character talks himself into the belief that, because he is so intellectually special and because he has good work in him that will "serve all mankind," he is entitled to steal from the local pawnbroker so as to pay his rent—leading to a double murder.

Do you possess this sense of entitlement?

If so, has it led to serious mischief?

Has it led to other unintended, negative consequences?

How might you go about honoring and safeguarding your intelligence without, at the same time, letting your sense of entitlement get you into trouble?

ENTRY 63

RUPTURES

This sense of entitlement can also lead to significant ruptures. For example, maybe that estrangement from your siblings or those past broken friendships can be traced back to this unfortunate dynamic? Has that maybe happened?

Can some of your ruptured relationships be traced back to you "lording it" over people?

Are there relationships of this sort that you'd like to repair?

____

____

____

____

____

____

How might you go about repairing them?

____

____

____

____

____

____

____

What are your headline thoughts on the subject of "a sense of entitlement"?

ENTRY 64

TORN APART

Another "high horse" challenge is using your ability to argue like a blunt instrument. One of the natural consequences of being smart is that you are able to argue well. You might be that lawyer whom everyone fears at trial, because you can tear apart any argument, catch witnesses in inconsistencies, and "make people believe anything." This may prove a wonderful asset at trial—but will it prove such a wonderful asset in your personal life?

Do you argue about everything? Are you that person who demands to hear the reasoning behind every minor decision that your mate makes, from why she bought white eggs rather than brown eggs to why she prefers sleeping with two pillows rather than one? Are you that person? And are you happy being that person?

Has it become your habit to argue about everything?

Do you find that that alienates and upsets the people around you?

Do you care that you are alienating or upsetting the people around you?

Is there anything about your "argumentative style," if that is your style, that you would like to change?

ENTRY 65

DEFEND YOURSELF!

A related challenge is making people defend their positions, as if they were on trial. For example, a person might routinely make the people around him feel as if they were being cross-examined. Do you shine a bright light on literally everything that other people say?

Is it your style to cross-examine the people with whom you interact?

Does that style serve you in your professional relationships?

Does that style serve you in your personal relationships?

Why do you consider it fair to cross-examine people?

ENTRY 66

THE BULLYING DEBATER

Related is the challenge of using your honed debating style to bully and criticize people. For example, someone who is passive-aggressive may not directly criticize the people around her, but she may still subtly criticize them by poking holes in their arguments and by bullying them with her biting wit.

Are you regularly critical of other people?

Are you in the habit of bullying people with your debating style?

Do you experience pleasure when you poke holes in another person's arguments?

Is there anything about your debating, bullying, or critical style that you would like to change?

ENTRY 67

I AM RIGHT!

Similarly, you may believe too strongly in your own opinions and too quickly reject the opinions of others. For example, a physicist might stake out his position on string theory or on the standard model and refuse to notice problems or inconsistencies with his position, defensively believing that, since he has adopted his position, it must be the right one.

When you stake out a position, is it almost impossible to move you from that position?

Can you think of a time when that stubbornness produced powerful negative consequences?

____

____

____

____

____

____

Would you like to be more tolerant and flexible, or do you prefer to adamantly stand behind your opinions and positions?

____

____

____

____

____

____

Do you see changing your mind as a sign of weakness?

ENTRY 68

THE HECK WITH GOOD WILL!

The last of these related challenges is relying on your argument style at the expense of fostering good will. For example, a person might conduct his business as if it were a zero-sum game, with only winners and losers, and use his debating skills to drive out competitors.

Would you prefer to win a debate, or would you prefer to foster good will?

Do you see good will as an encumbrance or weakness?

When you see that someone can't think quite as quickly as you can, do you see an opportunity to take advantage of them?

What are your insights about the relationship between your ability to argue well and your dealings with people?

ENTRY 69

COGNITIVE DECLINE

It isn't inevitable that your brain power decreases with age. Some people remain sharp as a tack as they age, but virtually everyone discovers that the way their brains operate changes over time, creating challenges to their usual ways of thinking. It is unlikely that you will be thinking "as well" at eighty as you were thinking at twenty. Whether or not everyone experiences cognitive decline with aging, certainly many people will and do.

Have you been experiencing cognitive decline? If so, how has it been manifesting?

How will the work you do be affected by any cognitive decline you might experience?

____

____

____

____

____

____

Are there any workarounds to help you deal with cognitive decline and its effects on your life and/or your work?

____

____

____

____

____

____

What have been the psychological effects of any cognitive decline you may be experiencing?

ENTRY 70

LOSS OF PRIDE

Along with the challenge that cognitive decline represents is the challenge of a loss of pride. One of the common psychological effects of cognitive decline can be wounded pride and a sense that you've become "less than" the person you'd always been.

Have you always taken pride in your cognitive abilities?

How has that pride manifested itself? In challenging yourself intellectually? In trying to solve knotty problems? In tackling large-scale creative work? In some other way?

Are you currently experiencing cognitive decline and a sense of wounded pride?

If you are, what might you like to try to do or think in order to ease the pain of that loss of pride?

ENTRY 71

LOSS OF IDENTITY

A loss of identity can also accompany cognitive decline. If one of your primary identities has always been "smart person," what will it feel like to slowly become a "less smart person"?

Have you long self-identified as a smart person? Has that been one of your primary identities, maybe even your prime self-identification?

Imagine losing that self-identification through cognitive injury or cognitive decline. How might you handle that loss?

How might you "rearrange" your identities in the face of such a loss? Might it be wise to adopt a "new identify" to replace that "smart person" identity? If so, what might you choose?

Picture yourself "wearing" that new identity. What do you see?

ENTRY 72

LACK OF MOTIVATION

Likewise, a lack of motivation can accompany cognitive decline. How motivated are you likely to feel to tackle your customary intellectual pursuits if it now feels too hard—or even impossible—to pursue them?

How might a lack of motivation to pursue your customary intellectual pursuits affect your motivation more generally?

What might you say to yourself to keep motivated in the face of cognitive decline?

What other tactics might you employ to keep yourself motivated in the face of cognitive decline?

Picture yourself still living actively and passionately in the face of cognitive decline. What do you see?

ENTRY 73

LOSS OF PURPOSE

A loss of purpose is also likely to accompany cognitive decline. If one of your more important life purposes was to do certain intellectual or creative work and now that has become harder or even impossible, will your other life purposes be able to "take up the slack"? Will you have to make a new investment in those other purposes or choose new ones?

If one or more of your life purposes are connected to your ability to think well, how might cognitive decline "rearrange" your understanding of your life purposes?

What tactics might you try in order to keep a felt sense of purpose afloat in the face of cognitive decline?

What inner language might you use in order to keep a felt sense of purpose afloat in the face of cognitive decline?

What are your overall thoughts, or headline thoughts, on the subject of cognitive decline?

ENTRY 74

RATIONALITY PLUS

On the one hand, a smart person knows that two plus two equals four. On the other hand, he is unlikely to find life satisfactorily explained by rationality alone. Life doesn't feel like the exact equivalent of mathematics and logic. But what is the plus? What is the more?

Do you find yourself in an unsettled relationship with rationality?

Do you have the sense that rationality is overrated or underrated...or both?

What, if anything, annoys you about the dictates of logic?

Do you have the sense that intuition is a function of, or different from, rationality?

ENTRY 75

EMOTIONS?

A smart person may wonder about the very legitimacy of emotions. Isn't the brain supposed to reign supreme? Isn't a hallmark of rationality the ability to control our emotions? On the other hand, don't emotions have their place? Is an ounce of love worth at least as much as a pound of chemical equations? What would an emotion-free life look like or feel like?

Do you find feelings suspect?

Are you upset when your emotions appear to be ruling the day?

Do your emotions sometimes cost you and sometimes serve you?

Describe the nature of the relationship you'd like to maintain with your emotions.

ENTRY 76

SMART AND CREATIVE

A smart person is not necessarily also a creative person. Indeed, many smart people have no desire to "be creative" and even scorn creativity as something arty, bohemian, indulgent, and pointless. Then there are smart people who would love to be more creative—only they don't know how to "get there." They can think well but feel stymied if asked to "think creatively" or if asked to "be creative." Is this you?

Are you smart but not currently creative? Why do you think that is?

How does "not being creative" play itself out in your life? What are the consequences for you of not feeling creative and/or not being creative?

What might you try so as to "increase" or "unleash" your creativity?

Picture yourself as a "more creative" person. What do you see?

ENTRY 77

SMARTNESS MADE REAL

The all-time-great chess player Bobby Fischer once remarked after one of his very few losses, "It's one thing to be a great chess player, and another thing to play a great game of chess." Likewise, it's one thing to be naturally smart and another thing to manifest that brain power. Just as a person with spring in her legs and the potential to jump high may never find a reason to jump high or the willingness to jump high, so a smart person may, for all sorts of reasons, never tackle an intellectual or creative challenge. For one person, that may prove just fine. For another person, however, that may amount to lifelong disappointment. Is this issue speaking to you?

Are you pretty certain that you haven't manifested or put into practice your natural smarts?

____

____

____

____

____

____

If so, is that okay or is that a problem?

____

____

____

____

____

____

____

If that is a problem, what do you think may be causing it?

If that is a problem, what do you think you might like to try to unleash your natural intelligence?

ENTRY 78

SMART AND WELL

Many smart, creative people do not lead lives that work for them. They discover that they aren't well emotionally, psychologically, physically, or existentially. My hope for you is that you do live well, which may require that you make changes and improvements to your life. Neither smartness nor creativity guarantee wellness: wellness is aspirational, and wellness is earned. I hope you aspire to it!

Is your life working?

What changes and improvements might help it work better?

Pick one of these changes or improvements. Paint a picture for yourself of how you might implement it.

Visualize implementing it. What do you see?

ENTRY 79

SMART AND WISE

Smart people do not always employ their native intelligence to help them live wisely. It is one thing to be smart; it is another thing to be wise. Many of our most talented, creative, and brilliant souls have succumbed to an addiction, lived lives of despair, committed suicide, or in other ways failed to find a peaceful life characterized by less self-sabotage and more ease and wisdom. My wish for you is that you find peace and lead with wisdom.

What sort of thing is wisdom? What do you take that word to mean?

Would you say that you are living a wise life?

If not, what might you try in order to live more wisely?

Picture yourself living a life of peace and wisdom. What do you see?

ENTRY 80

ALL THE REST OF LIFE

I hope that this journal has helped you think about, and focus on, some of the characteristic challenges that smart, sensitive, creative people face. But, of course, there are more challenges in life than the ones I've outlined. You may be challenged by a chronic health problem, by political turmoil, by a relationship gone sour, or some other all-too-human thing. Take this moment as an opportunity to bring forward any other challenge that may be confronting you.

Are one or two challenges that we haven't discussed currently confronting you?

Can you apply something you've learned from your reflections in this journal to those challenges?

Given the work that you've done in this journal, do you have a summary or headline reflection?

What do you see as your next steps in life?

AFTERWORD

I hope that you've benefited from thinking about the many issues that I've raised in this journal. Maybe you've even come to some important realizations and put into action some changes meant to address those challenges. That would be wonderful! At a minimum, I hope that you've found this journal thought-provoking and eye-opening. Congratulations on giving yourself the time, the space, and the opportunity to ponder these important issues.

You might want to dive more deeply into some of these matters. The first place to go would be to *Why Smart People Hurt*, the parent of this journal, which is out in a new edition with the title *Why Smart, Creative and Highly Sensitive People Hurt*. That book provides a much fuller discussion of the issues that I've raised in this journal and will prove an excellent resource as you continue your investigations.

Let me alert you to some other resources as well. I've discussed many of the themes raised in this journal in other books of mine. I've tackled the subject of anxiety in *Mastering Creative Anxiety* and *Performance*

Anxiety; addiction in *Creative Recovery*; depression in *Rethinking Depression* and *The Van Gogh Blues*; cognitive restructuring in *Write Mind* and *Redesign Your Mind*; living a creative life in *Fearless Creating*, *Coaching the Artist Within*, and *Unleashing the Artist Within*; healing and self-care in *Affirmations for Artists* and *Affirmations for Self-Love*; issues of personal safety in *Parents Who Bully* and *Overcoming Your Difficult Family*; and life purpose and meaning in *Life Purpose Boot Camp* and *Choose Your Life Purposes*.

I hope that these resources serve you. If you have any comments or questions, please feel free to be in touch with me at ericmaisel@hotmail.com. I look forward to hearing from you! And you can learn more about my books, coaching services, trainings, certificate programs, and other offerings at www.ericmaisel.com. I hope you enjoy your visit there.

ABOUT THE AUTHOR

Eric Maisel, a retired family therapist and active creativity coach, is the author of over fifty books and developer of the philosophy of life known as kirism.

In 2020, *Unleashing the Artist Within*, *The Creativity Workbook for Coaches and Creatives*, *Lighting the Way*, and *The Power of Daily Practice* appeared.

In 2021, *Transformational Journaling for Coaches, Therapists and Clients*, *The Great Book of Journaling*, and *Redesign Your Mind* appeared.

Dr. Maisel, widely regarded as America's foremost creativity coach, has writing extensively on the challenges of the creative life. His books in this area include *Fearless Creating*, *Coaching the Artist Within*, *Creative Recovery*, *The Van Gogh Blues*, and *Mastering Creative Anxiety*.

His books specifically for writers include *Deep Writing*, *Write Mind*, *Living the Writer's Life*, *A Writer's Space*, *A Writer's Paris*, and *A Writer's San Francisco*.

Dr. Maisel also writes extensively in the areas known as critical psychology and critical psychiatry, where he is a thought leader and advocate for significant shifts in mental health paradigms and practices.

His books in this area include *Rethinking Depression* (New World Library), *The Future of Mental Health* (Routledge), and *Humane Helping* (Routledge).

Among his other books for mental health professionals are *Helping Parents of Diagnosed, Distressed and Different Children, 60 Innovative Cognitive Strategies for the Bright, the Sensitive and the Creative*, and *Helping Survivors of Authoritarian Parents, Siblings and Partners*, all from Routledge.

Dr. Maisel leads workshops for writers online and around the world in locations like London, Paris, New York, San Francisco, Dublin, Rome, and Prague. He writes the "Rethinking Mental Health" blog for *Psychology Today* (with three million views) and three weekly blogs for *The Good Men Project*, including "Redesign Your Mind" and "Kirism Today."

Dr. Maisel trains creativity coaches, runs support groups for creativity coaches, and provides keynotes for organizations like the American Mental Health Counselors Association and the International Society for Ethical Psychology and Psychiatry. He divides his time between Walnut Creek, California, where he and his wife live, and Belmont, California, where his grandkid babysitting skills are required.

You can visit Dr. Maisel at www.ericmaisel.com, contact him at ericmaisel@hotmail.com, subscribe to his weekly newsletter at ericmaisel.com/newsletter, and be automatically notified about his new blog posts at authory.com/ericmaisel.

Mango Publishing, established in 2014, publishes an eclectic list of books by diverse authors—both new and established voices—on topics ranging from business, personal growth, women's empowerment, LGBTQ studies, health, and spirituality to history, popular culture, time management, decluttering, lifestyle, mental wellness, aging, and sustainable living. We were named 2019 *and* 2020's #1 fastest growing independent publisher by *Publishers Weekly*. Our success is driven by our main goal, which is to publish high-quality books that will entertain readers as well as make a positive difference in their lives.

Our readers are our most important resource; we value your input, suggestions, and ideas. We'd love to hear from you—after all, we are publishing books for you!

Please stay in touch with us and follow us at:

Facebook: Mango Publishing
Twitter: @MangoPublishing
Instagram: @MangoPublishing
LinkedIn: Mango Publishing
Pinterest: Mango Publishing
Newsletter: mangopublishinggroup.com/newsletter

Join us on Mango's journey to reinvent publishing, one book at a time.